The Savory Shellfish of North America

natural history   habitat   harvesting   recipes

By Sandra Romashko

Windward Publishing, Inc.
105 NE 25th St.   P.O. Box 371005   Miami, Fl. 33137

Other books by the author:
　　The Shell Book
　　The Shark Book
　　Living Coral
　　The Sportfisherman's Handbook
　　The Coral Book

Copyright © 1977 Sandra Romashko

ISBN 0-89317-015-1
Library of Congress No. 77-074610
1 3 5 7 9 11 13 15 17 19 20 18 16 14 12 10 8 6 4 2
Printed in the United States of America

Contents

Foreword 4
American Lobster 6
Spiny Lobster 11
Crawfish 14
Blue Crab 17
Dungeness Crab 23
King Crab 24
Stone Crab 28
Shrimp 31
Rock Shrimp 34
Abalone 37
Conch 39
Squid 41
Blue Mussel 43
Clams 45
Oysters 50
Scallops 57
Appendix, Shellfish Sauces 62
Index 63

Photo Credits:

Cover: Shellfish prepared and displayed by Mike Gordon, photography by Phil Brodatz.

State of Maine, Department of Marine Resources: 7, 44 bottom, 51.

The Miami Herald: 8.

Florida News Bureau: 12 bottom, 22, 29 bottom, 32 bottom, 33, 35, 36 bottom, 53, 57, 61 bottom.

Louisiana Department of Commerce and Industry: 15.

State of Maryland, Department of Economic and Community Development: 17, 19, 20, 21, 46, 54, 56.

Sea Library: 24, 37.

Guy C. Powell: 25.

Miami Seaquarium: 28, 40 top.

Bahamas News Bureau: 40 bottom.

NOAA, Southwest Region: 42.

Acknowledgements

I wish to thank the following people and organizations for their interest and cooperation in preparing materials for this book. Their sincere interest greatly helped in the research, but also made writing the book an enjoyable and pleasant task.

Guy C. Powell, Alaska Department of Fish and Game, Kodiak, Alaska. Bahamas News Bureau. Phil Brodatz, Miami, Florida. Florida Bureau of Marketing and Extension Services, Division of Marine Resources, Department of Natural Resources, Miami, Florida. Tim Olsson, State of Florida Department of Commerce, News Bureau, Tallahassee, Florida. Mike Gordon, Mike Gordon's Seafood Restaurant, Miami, Florida. Dr. Edwin S. Iversen, Rosenstiel School of Marine and Atmospheric Science, University of Miami, Florida. Cleo E. Gould, Louisiana Department of Commerce and Industry, Baton Rouge, Louisiana. Dan Kelly, State of Maine, Department of Marine Resources, Augusta, Maine. Gordon P. Hallock, State of Maryland, Department of Economic and Community Development, Seafood Marketing Authority, Annapolis, Maryland. The Miami Herald, Miami, Florida. The Sea Library, Santa Monica, California. Miami Seaquarium, Miami, Florida. U.S. Department of Commerce, National Oceanic and Atmospheric Administration, Southwest Region, Terminal Island, California. S.R.

Foreword

Shellfish are part of a large division of the animal kingdom called the invertebrates — animals without backbones. Invertebrates with three pairs of legs are insects and they comprise 70% of all the invertebrates. Those with more legs or none at all make up about 25% of the total number of invertebrates and include the majority of marine life including corals, sponges, starfish, worms, mollusks, and crustaceans. Those with more legs are classified as members of the phylum *Arthropoda,* class *Crustacea,* order *Decapoda* — invertebrates with ten legs including lobsters, crayfish, shrimp and crabs. Other invertebrates which have no true legs are classified in the phylum *Molluska* and include: (a) class *Gastropoda,* snails and single shelled mollusks; (b) class *Pelecypoda,* the bivalves, including oysters, clams, scallops, and mussels — mollusks with two shells; and (c) class *Cephalopoda* which includes squids, octopuses, and nautiluses.

Arthropods (Greek *arthron* = joint, Greek *podos* = foot) are characterized by having an external skeleton for support, hinged joints, and paired appendages. The crustaceans are further grouped by the common characteristics of two pairs of antennae, one pair jaws and two pairs of mouthparts. Those subclassified into the order *Decapoda* (Greek *deca* = ten, Greek *podos* = foot) have five pairs of walking legs.

Mollusks (Latin *mollis* = soft) are living animals which have a mantle of fleshy tissue which secretes lime to produce the mollusk's shell. Gastropods (Greek *gastrea* = belly, Greek *podos* = foot) have a single shell, a head, eyes, tentacles, and usually a radula – a file-like tongue coated with sharp teeth. They also have a single foot used for locomotion and many have an operculum on the back of the foot used to seal the shell when the animal is completely withdrawn. Those mollusks with two shells are called bivalves. The hinged ligament grows more slowly than the two shells which enlarge by concentric growths around the rim. Bivalves do not have a head or radula, but the burrowing species such as clams have a well developed foot. The cephalopods (Greek *kephale* = head, Greek *podos* = foot) are so named because they appear to have feet coming out of their head. In fact, the beak-like mouth is encircled by eight or more tentacles which are used to seize the prey.

This book is concerned with the edible decapods and mollusks that live in the water. Even though land varieties such as land crab *(e.g., cangrejo)* and land snails *(e.g., escargot)* are considered delicacies by many they are not included since they are not *water* shell*fish*. Jonathan Swift said, "He was a bold man that first eat an oyster." And a good thing that he did, or we might have missed these truly delectable offerings of the sea. Recipes follow each of the shellfish but they do not necessarily apply only to that particular shellfish. For example the clam chowder recipe can just as easily be conch chowder, squid chowder, or oyster stew by just substituting the appropriate shellfish. These substitutions are noted in the recipes.

Also included are tips on how to harvest the shellfish yourself. Freshly caught and eaten shellfish are usually far superior to those commercially available. However, BE SURE YOU CHECK WITH THE LOCAL DEPARTMENT OF HEALTH BEFORE YOU TAKE AND EAT SHELLFISH YOURSELF. Shellfish, particularly the mollusks, can cause serious illnesses if taken from polluted waters contaminated by waste or minute organisms.

Shellfish not only taste delicious but they are very healthful. They are high in protein and low in calories and cholesterol. So, go ahead, enjoy "The Savory Shellfish of North America."

American Lobster *Homarus americanus*

The American lobster, also called Maine lobster or New England lobster, is one of the most popular and well known of the shellfish. It is also probably the most expensive one to buy commercially. They are found along the Atlantic coast from the Maritime Provinces in Canada south to North Carolina and are most heavily concentrated in waters off Maine in the United States and Nova Scotia and Newfoundland in Canada. Lobsters are normally found in depths of 10-200 feet, but very large ones can be found in much deeper water. Commercial lobstermen set pots beyond the edge of the continental shelf in waters almost 2000 feet deep. The average size is 1-5 pounds, with some wily lobsters who survive to reach over 40 pounds. The large ones are tasty and do not become dry or tough in spite of their size. Personally, I find the tail meat to be the best consistency and most flavorful in a one pound "chicken" lobster.

In physical appearance the American lobster is almost identical to its freshwater counterpart, the crawfish. The upper part of the body is covered by a hard shell called the carapace. The lobster has 19 pairs of appendages: one pair small feelers which contain the sense of smell; one pair large feelers, the antennae, which are the sense of touch; one pair hard jaws used to grind food; five pairs of mouthparts used to hold the food; one pair large claws (which are really one of the five sets of legs in decapods) which capture food and are used as weapons; four pairs of walking legs; five pairs of swimmerets, one pair attached to each of the segments of the tail; one pair tail fans extending from the telson – the central portion of the last tail segment. Adults are colored greenish-blue to reddish-brown with the upper part of the body often marked with dark green spots. The shell only turns red after boiling.

Each of the large claws is slightly different. The larger claw – "crusher claw" – has strong blunt teeth, is club-like and used to crush the prey. The smaller and lighter claw – "quick claw" or "ripper claw" – has small sharp teeth and is used for lunging out and capturing prey. The big and small claw can be either on the left or right side with equal frequency. Those with only one claw are called "culls," and lobsters that have lost both claws are called "pistols."

Lobsters prefer dark and shady spots and often hide in crevices and holes during daylight. They are able to move quickly and feed primarily on small fish and invertebrates including mussels, clams, urchins, worms, and crabs. The lobster is a scavenger and will eat either dead or live prey. They feed more heavily as waters warm in spring and summer and will go into semi-hibernation in winter by burrowing in the mud and virtually stop eating. All are cannibalistic including the juveniles. Those in restaurant saltwater tanks have their claws taped or pegged so they don't attack and eat each other.

Sexual maturity is reached earlier in warm waters – a half-pound female (three or four years old) can be found carrying eggs. In colder waters they are often 2½ inches and 8-9 years old before they are mature. Mating occurs when the female

American lobster

has molted and is in a helpless state. The male, who has not molted, deposits sperm in receptacles in the female. The female will lay eggs from one month to one year after mating, but only once in a period of about two years. The eggs are fertilized as they are laid and pass over the sperm receptacles. The eggs have their own sticky adhesive which cements them into a pocket under the curved tail of the female. The number of eggs laid varies with the size of the females. The small ones lay about 5,000 while a large female may lay 10 times as many.

The female carries the fertilized eggs for 11-12 months until they hatch during the summer months in warmer areas or as late as September in cold waters. Hatching takes place over a 7-14 day period during which time the female shakes the ⅓ inch long young free from their egg cases. The young float with the water currents at the surface of the water for 3-5 weeks before they drop to the ocean floor to begin their normal life. They stay hidden until they reach a more secure size, 3-5 inches, before they enter deeper waters.

Growth is accomplished by molting – shedding the hard shell. The young begin to molt as early as their second day of life and continue to molt for the rest of their lives. Rate of growth is faster in warm waters, but on the average a six inch lobster is three years old, a nine inch lobster is about 4½ years old, which is the average size at maturity. After reaching maturity, the male grows much faster than the female since the female does not molt while she is carrying eggs – a period of a year. In both sexes the rate of growth decreases with age.

Most states require a license for both commercial and sport lobstermen. Legal size in most states is 3-3/16 inches from eye sockets to end of carapace. (Short,

7

A twenty-pound American lobster

Wooden slat lobster pot

illegal size lobsters are called "snappers" or "shorts.") Some states set a maximum limit of five inches because larger lobsters lay more eggs. Trapping is normally done in a lobster "pot" – a crate or wooden box which is generally oblong and has one or more netted funnel-like openings. Lobsters pass from the outside through the wide end of the opening into the trap to get the bait in the "kitchen." After eating, the lobster looks for a way out, and the easiest exit is another opening of the pot which leads to a rear chamber, "the parlor." The bait remains on the spike in the "kitchen" to tempt another lobster. The pot is weighted down with bricks or weights and any fresh, salted or stale fish can be used as bait. The traps are marked by floats or buoys tied to them. Pots may break loose and be lost and become "ghost pots." They usually will have one lobster in them – the survivor who ate all the others he was trapped with after the bait was eaten. The giant lobsters do not fit in pots and are taken by divers. Divers may legally take lobster in Massachusetts, but not in New Hampshire or Maine.

Commercial dragger lobstermen employ another method of harvesting lobster. A purse-like net is dragged on rollers across the bottom. Larger lobsters are caught this way but many are killed or mutilated by this method.

"Farmers" have attempted to raise lobsters in captivity. However the cannibalistic lobsters must be kept separate. Biologists have been able to increase the growth rate more than three times by raising lobster in 70° waters. The lobsters in this environment reach one pound in less than two years.

The lobster is threatened by over-fishing and pollution. Ninety per cent of all legal size lobsters are taken every year.

PREPARATION AND RECIPES

Fresh, whole lobster should be live, and exhibit motion. "Green" lobster is best when a whole lobster is frozen live. This protects the meat from drying out. ("Green" applies to any decapod which is frozen, *uncooked,* in the shell). Fresh frozen "green" lobster will keep for a period of four months without any loss in quality. Frozen cooked lobster in the shell is best used within two months. To kill a live lobster, plunge a sharp knife into the thorax or center part of the lobster at the point where the body and tail meet.

1. Steamed Lobster

Use a steamer with a rack at the bottom and add about one inch of water to the pot. After water has come to a rolling boil, put lobsters in pot head first. Cover tightly. Steam 10 minutes for one-pound lobsters, 15 minutes for two-pound lobsters, 20 minutes for three-pounders, etc. After cooking, cut the body and tail in half lengthwise and remove and discard the tough sac located behind the eyes. Serve with melted butter.

2. Clam Bake

For each person:

1 chicken lobster	1 piece chicken
6 clams	1 ear of corn
1 small onion	clam juice
1 potato	

If potato is large, partially bake the potato and soak corn in water ahead of time. Place all ingredients in heavy duty aluminum foil making an individual packet for each person. Add ½ cup clam juice to each packet before sealing. Cook in oven or outdoor cooker for one hour, turning packets every 15 minutes. Serve with melted butter.

3. Authentic New England Clam Bake

Dig a hole two feet deep and any convenient length and width. A 2 foot x 4 foot x 2 foot hole will cook a clam bake for up to 30 people.

Line bottom with rocks which are 3-5 inches in diameter. Start a wood fire over the tops of the rocks, keeping the fire burning for 5 hours. Rake all the embers off the rocks. Add a full 2 inch layer of seaweed over the rocks. (All references to seaweed in this recipe call for wet, saltwater seaweed). Add a layer of whole, live lobster – allow 3 chicken lobsters per couple – and cover with 1-2 inches of seaweed. Next add a layer of raw, whole new potatoes and chicken halves (optional). Again cover with a layer of 1-2 inches seaweed. Add a layer of soft-shell clams (it may be handy to support small clams with screening) and cover with a full 2 inches of seaweed. Cover the hole with a wet canvas tarpaulin, weighting the tarp down with rocks. After 1 hour the "bake master" reaches in for a clam. If clam is open and succulent, the bake is finished. Otherwise, continue checking every 10 minutes until bake is done. Serve portions in peach basket. Serve melted butter in disposable cups – deep enough to dip the ears of corn and the lobster. Serve with beer and lots of napkins. The traditional dessert is ice cold watermelon.

Spiny lobster can be substituted for American lobster in these recipes. Also see Recipes **4, 5, 9, 12** which can be made with lobster.

Spiny Lobster   *Panulirus argus*

The clawless spiny lobster derives its name from its heavy antennae which are covered with hundreds of pointed spines. Since it lacks claws these antennae are the lobster's main weapon. There are six species of spiny lobster in the western Atlantic of which *P. argus* is the most important. The lobster is found in the Atlantic waters from North Carolina to Bermuda, south to Brazil. They are found in southern Gulf of Mexico and the Caribbean with heavy concentrations in south Florida, the Bahamas, Cuba and British Honduras. Relatives of spiny lobster are found in California waters, in the Mediterranean, and waters off South Africa and Australia.

Also sometimes called sea crawfish or Florida lobster, the spiny lobster is marked with brown, yellow, orange, green and blue on both the upper and under sides of the tail. They have jointed shells, antennae, and legs. The five pairs of legs contain chemically responsive receptors which enable the lobster to "taste." The tail is segmented and can be curled beneath the lobster, enabling him to move backward rapidly. The lobster's usual direction of movement is either forward or sideways. The spiny lobster may reach 20 pounds and live as long as 25 years, but any individuals over five pounds are rare.

Sexually mature spiny lobsters usually are 8-9 inches long. Females may breed twice each season, during the periods of February-April and June-July. The female has a spermatophore at the base of her leg. The brilliant orange eggs are passed from oviducts on the third pair of legs, over the spermatophore to be fertilized and are attached and incubated under the female's tail. Two to three weeks after mating, the larvae hatch – they are called phyllosomas. The larvae drift with the current, feeding on plankton. They may molt as much as eleven times before they become infant lobsters which then settle to the bottom, molting less and less often as they grow older. Even though 2-2.5 million eggs are fertilized at one time, very few larvae survive.

The spiny lobster feeds at night and likes to hide in ledges and crevices. The lobster eats clams, conchs, urchins, hermit crabs, sea cucumbers, starfish, its own young and dead fish. They are usually taken in waters less than 30 feet deep, but they migrate up to 100 miles to deeper waters during cold weather and at certain times in spring, long parades of hundreds of lobsters march single file from shallow to deep waters. Spiny lobsters grow by molting, but normally only molt after they have been well fed.

Spiny lobster

Spiny lobsters are commercially harvested in wooden pots in Florida waters.

All species are good to eat. Commercially they are harvested by both wooden-slat and wire pots, and hoopnets. They are harvested by hand by divers.

The spiny lobster is protected in Florida waters. Legal season lasts from August 1 through March 31. At no time can egg carrying females be taken. Legal size is a minimum three inch carapace or minimum 5½ inch tail length. Sportsmen should familiarize themselves with the strict regulations which regulate the harvesting of spiny lobster. It is illegal to molest commercial lobster traps.

PREPARATION AND RECIPES

If spiny lobster is purchased live, it should show movement. Normally the lobster is commercially available in the frozen "green" form, frozen cooked whole lobster, or frozen cooked tails. Cooked lobster is easily recognized since the shell turns red-orange in color. "Green" lobster is best when a whole lobster is frozen live with the shell intact to prevent the meat from drying out. Fresh frozen "green" lobster will keep for a period of four months without any loss in quality. Frozen cooked lobster in the shell is best when used within two months.

To prepare raw or cooked lobster, lay lobster on its back and with a sharp knife cut lobster in half lengthwise. Remove both the stomach from the body section and the intestinal vein which runs from the stomach to the tip of the tail. Rinse body cavity thoroughly. If lobster is live, place live lobster in the freezer for 20 to 30 minutes which makes it easier to handle when splitting the lobster. After cleaning,

Bahamian youth shows off two large spiny lobsters

lobster can be cooked in the shell. To remove meat, use a sharp knife to loosen the meat from the edges of the shell and pick the meat up with a fork at the tip of the tail, lifting upward and pulling the meat toward the head away from the shell.

4. Baked Stuffed Lobster

2 cleaned in the shell lobsters 2 tablespoons melted margarine or butter
1½ cups soft bread crumbs 1 tablespoon grated onion
½ cup grated cheddar cheese paprika

Combine bread crumbs, cheese, butter and onion. Place stuffing in body cavity and spread over surface of the tail meat. Sprinkle with paprika. Place on a baking pan, 15" x 10" x 1." Bake in hot oven, 400° F, for 15-20 minutes or until lightly browned. Serve with melted butter and lemon wedges.

5. Broiled Lobster

Remove the liver and coral from cleaned split lobster in shell. Mix with ½ cup cracker crumbs, salt and pepper to taste, ¼ cup melted butter. Broil lobster, shell side up, for 6 minutes. Turn, spread mixture on flesh side, and broil 6 more minutes. Serve with melted butter and lemon wedges.

American lobster can be substituted for spiny lobster in these recipes. Also see Recipes **1, 2, 3, 6, 9, 12** which can be made with spiny lobster.

Crawfish *Procambarus* sp.

Crawfish, crayfish, or crawdad — all interchangeable names — are found in freshwater on all continents of the world except Africa. There are more than 300 species worldwide of which 100 species are common to the United States. The state of Louisiana alone has 29 species. The American crawfishes fall into five common genera: *Pacifasticus,* found in Canada, Alaska, Mexico, Pacific Coast of United States to the Rocky Mountains; *Procambarus,* Cuba, Guatemala, Honduras, Mexico, Mississippi Valley and southeastern United States; *Cambarus* are found from the Gulf of Mexico north to Canada; *Orconectes,* found in Mississippi and Great Lakes drainage systems; and *Cambarellus,* found in the southern United States.

Crawfish very closely resemble the American lobster in appearance, and have identical appendages, 19 pairs, on the segmented body. Species vary in size and color from one inch to 16 inches at maturity. They can be colored light tan to dark with various shades of yellow, blue, red and green. Habits also vary depending on species. Some spend all of their lives burrowed underground; some burrow only under conditions of drought or during the reproductive cycle. Still other species never burrow but spend their lives in puddles, ponds, ditches and various streams and lakes. The average life span is 1-3 years. Females produce from 15-700 young yearly.

There are two predominant crawfishes in Louisiana: the red swamp crawfish *P. clarki* and white river crawfish *P. blandingi acutus*. Peak breeding season for these species is late May, early June in open water. The males deposit sperm into an external receptacle on the female. Sperm are held until eggs are laid during September-October. However spawning will occur at irregular intervals during flooding or dry spells. In June most crawfish ponds are drained and the females burrow into the mud at this time. Males may burrow or merely dig into the mud. Egg laying starts in September. If the pond is dry the eggs are laid in the burrows. As the eggs are laid they are simultaneously fertilized by the sperm held in the receptacle and adhere to the underside of the tail with a sticky substance called glair. The eggs hatch in 14-29 days with the peak hatching period occurring in October. If water is plentiful the young become "free swimmers" and begin immediately to feed and grow. If water is not present, the young are released in the burrows and due to lack of food and crowding, they do not grow. Or the female may release the young on land and they will either die from dehydration or be captured by predators. Under optimum conditions, young crawfish will develop to market size in 60-90 days. The best temperature for growth is 70°-85° F; tempera-

Fresh water crawfish

15

tures below 45° drastically reduce growth. Low oxygen content in a pond will also retard growth. This situation can be caused by the presence of large amounts of decaying matter in the pond.

Crawfish eat living and dead plant and animal matter. They prefer fresh meat – bait that is decaying does not attract them. Twenty percent of their natural diet includes worms, larvae; the balance is vegetation. Crawfish also eat clover, alfalfa, Bermuda grass, sorghum, and aquatic plants. Fish, crows, bullfrogs, raccoons, mink and wading birds are the natural enemies of the crawfish.

Crawfish are commercially farmed in three types of ponds: (1) rice ponds – crawfish and rice crops are alternated; (2) open ponds; (3) wooded or swampland ponds. Funnel traps and "drop" nets are used to harvest the crawfish in the ponds. Harvesting is normally best if water temperature is above 60° F.

Wild areas are fished with ¾ inch mesh chickenwire traps. These traps are usually 30-36 inches long so they can be propped with a small portion of one end exposed above the water allowing the crawfish to breathe and stay alive. Many baits are used including fish heads, cut shad, perforated cans of dog food.

Sportsmen use crawfish nets to catch crawfish. These nets are cord-woven ½ inch mesh squares joined at each end by inverted "V" sections of wire or coathangers. A loop joins the tops of the inverted "V's." The best bait for the nets is "melt" – beef pancreas – which is tied to the bottom of the net. Louisiana has no season or limit for harvesting crawfish. In Oregon – second only to Louisiana as a commercial producer – the season is open throughout the year but limits are sometimes set. The state of Washington requires a commercial permit and has fixed crawfish regulations which must be followed. The crawfish can only be taken in shellfish pots and must be a minimum length of 3¼ inches; season varies depending on section.

Crawfish are similar to the American lobster in texture and taste. High quality crawfish are those which are greater than 3½ inches from tip of the tail to the tip of the head, weigh 15-25 per pound, and have bright yellow fat. This size will produce 15-18 pounds of tail meat for every 100 pounds of live crawfish.

PREPARATION AND RECIPE

Wash live crawfish in large tub of water and remove and discard twigs, vegetation and dead crawfish. Purge the crawfish by soaking them in a strong salt water solution for five minutes.

6. Boiled Crawfish

15 pounds washed and purged crawfish	1 or 1½ boxes salt
	cayenne pepper
6 lemons	3 heads of garlic
4 red onions	commercial seafood boil

Fill a pot with enough water to cover the crawfish. Add salt to taste but enough so that the water is well salted; add pepper to your taste. Cut the lemons, onions and garlic and add to water along with seafood boil added according to their instructions. Cover the pot and bring to a good boil, then add the crawfish and bring to a second boil. Boil for 3-5 minutes depending on size of the crawfish. Turn off fire and let crawfish soak in hot seasoned water for 20-30 minutes or longer until the meat is sufficiently seasoned to your taste.

Spiny lobster can be substituted for crawfish in this recipe.

Blue Crab   *Callinectes sapidus*

The blue crab is the most important commercial crustacean with the exception of Maine lobster and shrimp. It is the most popular of all the edible crabs and about 75% of all crabs marketed in the United States are blue crabs. It is a member of the *Portunidae* family of swimming crabs which are characterized by having their fifth

Blue crabs

(last) pair of legs flattened like paddles for swimming. The first pair of legs end in long pointed claws. The front part of the oval shell has several sharp "teeth-like" protrusions and the lateral tips are elongated into sharp spines. The color ranges from dark-blue or blue-green to mottled brown on the top with a cream colored underside. Their usual direction of movement is sideways, they may reach eight inches across in size and live 3½ years. But most live less than a year, and average 5-7 inches across the shell.

Blue crabs are found in Atlantic waters from Cape Cod to Florida, and in the Gulf of Mexico. Occasionally they can even be found at the far extremes of Nova Scotia and Uruguay. In Europe, blue crabs are found in the waters of France, Holland and Denmark.

The crabs live in salt water but are found most abundantly in muddy bays and in estuaries. During warm weather they can be found inshore. Although they are active throughout the year, in cold weather they move to deeper waters and exist in a state of semi-hibernation.

In the middle Atlantic the spawning season is from May to October with the peak in late August-early September. Blue crabs mate inshore in brackish waters and the eggs are laid in June, July, August, a period of 2-9 months after mating. The egg carrying females are called sponge crabs, berry crabs or cushion crabs. It is illegal to harvest egg bearing females which can be recognized by the large orange mass of eggs protruding from beneath the apron. The newly laid eggs are bright orange. Males may mate with more than one female and females may spawn twice during the same season. The females may lay ¾ to 2 million eggs, of which only a few survive to adulthood. The female blue crab can be distinguished from the male by the shape of the apron. The female has a rounded apron with a short extension; the male has a longer extension on the apron.

Larval crabs molt several times, changing shape with each molt until they reach adult form in about a month. Young and juvenile blue crabs grow very quickly and reach adult size within 1 to 1½ years. The molted blue crab is the principal source of "soft-shell" crab.

The blue crab will eat anything – fresh and dead meat, plants, seaweed, decomposing grass and seaweed. In turn they are eaten by several fishes, including cobia which regularly feed on them.

Commercial fishermen use dredges, trawls, nets, pots, seines, and dipnets to harvest blue crabs. Some sportsmen use crab pots, but most use meshed nets baited and marked with floats, or tied to pilings, piers or bushes. The crab pots vary in design, but all are based on the same principle. An inner compartment holds the bait and allows the crab to enter through several openings; the openings do not allow easy escape.

Soft-shell crabs are commercially harvested in "brush traps" – clumps of branches suspended from a trotline. These traps work because a molting crab seeks shelter in which to hide while the new shell is in the process of hardening. Or, other commercial fishermen hold hard-shell crabs and watch for those who are about to molt and then transfer them to other pens until they have molted. Newly molted soft-shells are refrigerated or frozen immediately to retard hardening of the shell.

Clam bake Maryland style – use blue crabs instead of lobster.

PREPARATION AND RECIPES

Blue crabs are commercially available in both the hard-shell and soft-shell stages. Soft-shell crabs are available fresh or frozen, but in the latter case they should be solidly frozen when purchased. Hard-shell crabs are sold alive or as cooked meat, either fresh or pasteurized. Blue crab meat does not freeze well so pasteurization is used to prolong the shelf life of the meat. The process does not alter the taste or texture of the meat, but it does prolong the shelf life – an unopened can may be stored under refrigeration for six months. Crabs that are purchased alive must show movement. Fresh crabmeat is best if used within two days and keeps better if packed on ice in the refrigerator. Pasteurized crabmeat must be kept under refrigeration. If you wish to freeze your own crabmeat, freeze it

19

raw after removing the claws and inner pod of cartilage which contains the meat, discarding the rest of the crab. Freeze the uncracked claws and unpicked pod of meat whole in a container filled with water and freeze until a solid block of ice is formed.

How to clean a blue crab. (1) Lay the crab upside down and lift the flap (apron) pulling it back and down to remove the top shell. Remove the gills, intestines and spongy matter from the top side of the crab. (2) Pull legs loose from the body and

Commercial crab pot used to harvest blue crabs

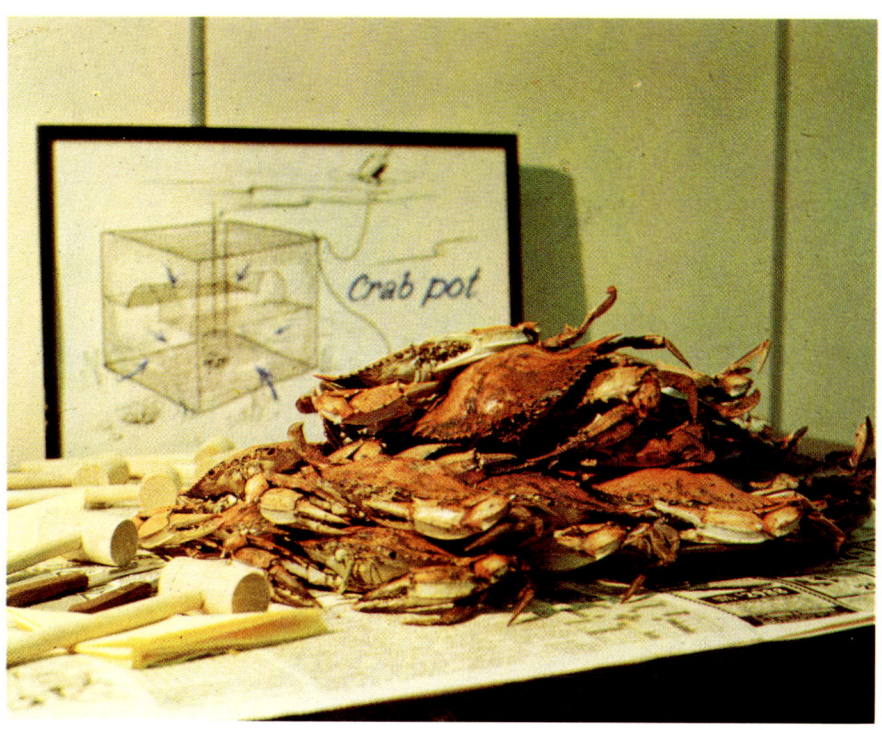
Steamed blue crabs

break off the claws. (3) Cut off the top of the inner skeleton and remove all exposed meat. (4) The back of the crab, on each side, contains a large lump of white meat which can be removed in one lump by cutting it out with a knife. (5) Remove the white flake meat with the point of a knife or other pointed instrument. (6) Crack the claws and remove the meat. If you are eating whole steamed crabs, you can remove the meat from the legs by putting the leg at its joint between your teeth and drawing the shell between your teeth while sucking out the meat.

7. Steamed Blue Crabs

½ cup commercial seafood boil seasoning
½ cup salt
3 cups white vinegar
3 cups beer (or water)
3 dozen live crabs
cayenne pepper (optional)

You may anesthetize the live crabs by putting them in a sink or large container and running hot tap water over them. This makes the crabs easier to handle. Scrub the crabs with a vegetable brush to remove any mud from shells. Using a steamer pot with a rack and tight fitting lid, fill the pot with water to just below the rack. Thoroughly mix the seasonings, vinegar and beer (or water), and the cayenne pepper to taste if a spicier boil is preferred. Put one half of the crabs in the pot and pour one half of the seasoned mixture over the top, add the remaining crabs and remaining mixture. Steam, covered, until crabs turn bright red in color, about 20-30 minutes. Serve over newspapers with wooden mallets. Serve with melted butter or mustard sauce if you like.

8. **Fried Soft-shell Crabs**

To prepare soft-shells for cooking, wash them several times. Place crab right side up and make a cut just behind the eyes and remove the face. Lift the tapered points on either side of the shell and remove the sandbags and spongy gills. Turn crab over on back and remove the pointed apron with a knife. Dry crabs and sprinkle with salt and pepper. Coat lightly with flour if desired. Fry in pan with just enough fat to keep crabs from sticking. Fry until browned, about 5 minutes on each side. Or, deep fry at 375° F for 2-3 minutes or until browned.

Florida crabman harvests blue crab — the most popular species of all edible crabs in the U.S.

Dungeness Crab *Cancer magister*

The Dungeness crab is a member of a group of crabs all of genus *Cancer* which commonly share the characteristic of living only in salt water. There are 19 species worldwide, and all of them live in the temperate zone. Dungeness crabs are found in shallow, sandy waters along the Pacific coast from the Alaskan peninsula to Mexico and are the basis for important commercial fisheries in Oregon, Washington, Alaska, California and British Columbia.

The carapace (upper shell) is colored reddish brown and the underside is white. Males grow larger than females to a maximum carapace width of nine inches and they may live 8-10 years. They reach market size (over six inches) in 4½ years. They grow by molting and newly molted Dungeness crabs are very active. A true crab, the Dungeness moves sideways and can replace lost appendages.

The female can be distinguished from the male by the shape of the abdomen. The female crab has a semi-circle shaped abdomen and several pairs of abdominal appendages; the male has a triangular shaped abdomen and only two pairs of appendages.

Sexual maturity is reached in the female at a size of about 4 inches. Depending on location, mating occurs from April or May until as late as September. Mating takes place on tide flats, between soft-shelled (newly molted) females and hard-shelled males. The sperm are deposited in a sperm receptacle in the female. Eggs develop within the female's ovaries, changing color from white to red as they increase in size. The eggs are fertilized as they are laid and are attached to the abdominal appendages to develop. Females can produce 3-5 million eggs in three or four broods during their lifetime. Hatching takes place during the period of December-June. The larvae are pelagic and live at the surface of the water for a period of three months passing through six development stages.

The crab's usual foods include oysters, cockles, and small fish. However, clams, birds, salmon heads, and chicken entrails make excellent bait. Commercially, they are harvested primarily in crab pots and hoop nets. Crabbing is regulated in all areas by law and the rules regarding sex and size of legal Dungeness vary with the local enforcement agencies.

PREPARATION AND RECIPE

Procedures for freezing and holding Dungeness crab are the same as those listed for the blue crab. Cleaning and preparing the Dungeness crab is essentially the same as the blue crab except that the Dungeness crab has much more body meat and is 2-3 times larger than the blue crab.

9. Crab Louis

Place live crabs in boiling salted water (⅓ cup salt per 6 quarts water). Cover and return to the boiling point. Reduce heat and simmer 15-20 minutes. Rinse under cold water. Remove meat from crab and cool.

Dungeness crabs   Photo Steve Williams

Place 2 cups cooled crab meat in 4 bowls over lettuce. Pour over **Louis Dressing:** mix together 1 cup mayonnaise, ¼ cup whipping cream, ¼ cup chili sauce, 1 teaspoon Worcestershire sauce (optional), ¼ cup chopped green pepper, ¼ cup chopped green onion, 1-2 tablespoons lemon juice, season to taste with salt and pepper. Sliced, hard cooked eggs may be added. Sprinkle with chopped chives.

Any crab meat, shrimp, or scallops may be substituted for Dungeness crab in this recipe.

King Crab   *Paralithodes camtschatica*

The king crab, also called Alaskan king crab, is found on the North American coast from the northern tip of Vancouver Island north into Bristol Bay and to the edge of the Bering Sea ice pack. On the Asian coast, king crab is found from the Sea of Japan north to the Sea of Okhotsk and along Kamchatka Peninsula. In Alaska the main concentration of crab lies off the Alaskan peninsula, Aleutian Islands, Kodiak Island and Cook Inlet.

King crab　　　　　　　　　　　　　　　　　　　　Photo Guy C. Powell

Pod of juvenile king crabs　　　　　　　　　　　　Photo Guy C. Powell

Like its relatives, the king crab has five pairs of legs although only four are usually visible. The fifth pair of legs is much smaller and is tucked out of sight underneath the bottom shell. The first pair of legs ends in claws. The great claw is very strong and the crab can break a finger in it. The king crab is not a true crab but belongs to a separate group that includes the hermit crab. The normal direction for walking is diagonally, not sideways as other crabs.

King crabs can reach great size — the largest on record had a leg spread of almost five feet and weighed over 24 pounds. It is not uncommon to find kings three feet across and weighing 10 pounds. They prefer fresh food, but they eat a wide variety including crabs, starfish, sea cucumbers, sand dollars. King crabs can live as long as 18 years, with a rare member reaching a maximum of 25 years.

Molting is the means of growth in all crustaceans. One to two weeks before a molt, the color of the king crab changes from dull red to dark brown and it becomes inactive. The new shell has begun to develop within the old, separated by a colorless lubricant between the two shells. Three days before the molt the abdomen swells. Slowly, the area between the abdomen and carapace splits and gradually the legs, body, head and eyes ease out of the old shell. It takes a crab 10-20 minutes, depending on size, to shed an old shell.

King crabs mature at about 5-6 years of age. They mate and spawn annually in shallow water. The males, followed by the females, migrate into shallow waters where the male searches out a female who is about to molt. He claims the female by grabbing her front legs with his claws so they are face to face and they remain holding hands until the female molts, sometimes for a period of 2-3 weeks. If the male wants to move, he raises the female over his head as he moves across the ocean floor. The male may bounce the female on the bottom, apparently in an attempt to speed up the molting process. After the female has molted, the male spreads his sperm across her oviduct openings. Eggs are formed and fertilized, remaining as clusters on tiny hairs which cover small appendages under the female's abdomen.

The female incubates the fertilized eggs for 11 months in the brood pouch under her abdomen. The area is formed by the horny apron of the abdominal flap. Depending on size, she may carry as many as 50,000 to 400,000 eggs. At hatching time the female migrates to shallow waters. Raising herself on the long legs, she drops open her flap and shakes the larvae free of the eggs. The newly hatched larvae are 1/32 inch long. The young swim freely for 6-8 weeks, changing shape during several molts while growing into a recognizable king crab shape at 1/16 inch across. At the final stage, the free-floating larvae drop to the ocean floor where they remain for the rest of their lives.

Juvenile king crabs occupy shallow waters for 2-3 years. During their first year they molt about eight times reaching a size of approximately ½ inch across. During the next year and four more molts they reach one inch across. Young two and three year old crabs accumulate in groups called pods, which may include as many as 3000 male and female crabs. The crabs stand on each other's backs, all facing in the same direction, forming a pile shaped like an umbrella or a basketball. The pod disbands to feed or to change directions, then they reassemble. The formation of pods is apparently an application of the "strength in numbers" adage, since young individuals are easy prey for any other sea animal.

After reaching 3-4 years, the king crabs move to deep waters, 120-240 feet deep in summer or as far as 600 feet deep in winter. After 4-6 years, the males molt once a year, growing an inch per molt until approximately the sixth or seventh year when molting can occur only once in 2-3 years.

The commercial crab fishing industry was practically zero in the 1940's but has grown to about 40% of the size of the salmon industry in Alaska. They are caught in commercial crab pots, 7 feet square x 2½ feet deep, made of welded steel-rod frames covered with heavy nylon mesh. The traps are baited with halibut heads and herring. The traps weigh 700 pounds and are raised and lowered by hydraulic lifts. The traps rest on the bottom for 2-3 days before being lifted on board the commercial ships where holding tanks can carry 12,000 crabs and keep them alive for over a month.

After raising the pots, the king crabs are sorted. All females are released (distinguished by their smaller size and shape of the bottom shell) and male "keepers" must be seven inches – a 7-10 year old crab – or more across the carapace. King crabs are most easily caught during their migration into shallow waters to spawn.

Japanese and Russian fishermen take crabs with tangle nets. These nets are 150 feet long and eight feet high and are anchored in strings of 20-35 nets. The nets are weighted at the bottom and buoyed at the top producing a net wall which snares and entangles the crabs. The nets are lifted to the "picker boats" where the crabs are picked off the nets with little metal hooks. Tangle nets are prohibited to U.S. fishermen.

The Japanese have fished king crabs since the 1880's and fished the Bering Sea as early as 1930. Americans thought they were after salmon, but the knowledge that they were taking crab started a new industry in America. In 1968, the United States declared the Alaskan king crabs to be "creatures of our continental shelf" and thus the property of the United States. Japan and the U.S.S.R. have continued fishing under quotas. Due to the quotas, the more abundant and smaller snow crabs are often substituted for king crab in Japan, but they are relatively unknown on U.S. tables.

PREPARATION AND RECIPE

King crab is commercially available frozen in cans or as whole par-boiled frozen legs. The legs can be thawed and steamed and served in the shell – cut the shell down the center – with melted butter.

10. Crab Au Gratin

1½ pounds crab meat, cut into chunks
¼ cup chopped green onions or shallots
¼ cup butter or margarine
1 cup light cream
salt
pepper
¼ cup grated Parmesan cheese

Saute crab chunks, and onions or shallots in butter for 5 minutes. Add cream, salt and pepper to taste and heat thoroughly. Put mixture into 4 oven-proof serving dishes and sprinkle tops with Parmesan cheese. Bake at 350° F for 5 minutes.

Any crab meat can be substituted for king crab in this recipe.

Stone Crab *Menippe mercenaria*

The stone crab is found in Atlantic and Gulf of Mexico waters from North Carolina to Texas, with the largest concentration in Florida. However, even in Florida, the stone crab is outnumbered by the blue crab. The stone crab is a member of the mud-crab family, *Xanthidae*, characterized by the oval-shaped flattened shell.

The crab has large powerful black tipped claws which can inflict a severe bite. The body color ranges from purplish to dark or reddish brown with brown mottlings. The sharp-pointed legs are fringed with hair and are marked by red and yellow bands. The bulky looking shell is very hard and heavy. Stone crabs reach five inches across the tips of the shell and about two inches in body thickness.

Stone crabs burrow in deep holes of mud and sand and are found near creeks, estuaries, under rocks and on mangrove roots. They are difficult to take by hand,

Stone crab

Stone crab claws

Commercial crabman sets pots in Apalachicola, Florida

so crab pots, iron hooks, hook and line are used. They are fished commercially in Beaufort, N.C.; Charleston, S.C.; Miami, Naples and Key West, Florida. Only the claws are available commercially and the rich, white, solid claw meat is similar to the claws of the American lobster.

Popular opinion credits *Joe's Stone Crab Restaurant* in Miami Beach as the pioneer in preparing and serving stone crab. In 1915 the original Joe's was operated as a small restaurant on the front porch of Joe Weiss' home. The restaurant started out with six tables and has grown since then to the large popular restaurant run by Jesse Weiss and Irwin Sawitz, and the success story is undeniably attributed to the stone crab.

Developer Jim Allison hired a Harvard icthyologist to classify marine life in Biscayne Bay. The professor saw young boys catching crabs and thought they looked edible since they resembled the delicious Cuban Moro crab. He and Allison tried them; they thought they were good but had a strange taste. Allison took some to "Joe's"; Joe boiled them, chilled them and later tasted them. The chilling firmed up the meat and destroyed any taste of the iodine. So in 1923 Joe put a cauldron in the back yard and started selling stone crab. Thus *Joe's Stone Crab Restaurant* began and has won *Holiday's* award for dining every year since 1961.

Florida game laws allow only one claw of the stone crab to be taken, and then the crab must be returned to the water alive. The claw must be broken carefully at the "breaking joint" so as not to rupture the shell. If the crab is returned to the water with the shell intact and the claw properly removed, he will survive and replace the missing claw, provided he is also left with one claw to defend himself. Legal size for the claw is a minimum 2¾ inch forearm. The stone crab season is closed from May 15 through October 15, when the crabs molt and spawn.

PREPARATION AND RECIPE

The claws are boiled in seawater immediately upon landing and then held iced until served. Freezing or icing raw crab claws causes the meat to stick to the inside of the shell. Cooked stone crab claws can be frozen in the shell, but freeze only claws that are completely intact to prevent deterioration of the meat. Freshly cooked and frozen claws can be kept for six months and should be thawed in the refrigerator for 12-18 hours to prevent loss of quality. Freshly cooked claws can be kept for 2-3 days if packed on ice and refrigerated at 32°F to 35°F.

11. Stone Crabs with Mustard Sauce

To serve claws, crack each section with hammer or flat side of metal meat tenderizer. Do not *smash* meat. (Most people prefer cold stone crab claws, but they can also be served resteamed until heated and served with melted butter.) Serve cold stone crab claws with mustard sauce.

Mustard Sauce: Combine ½ cup sour cream; 1½ tablespoons prepared mustard; 2 teaspoons melted butter or margarine; ½ teaspoon parsley flakes; ⅛ teaspoon salt. Heat all ingredients at a low temperature, until just warm, stirring occasionally. Do not boil.

Shrimp Family *Penaeidae*

Shrimp can be found in both fresh and salt water all around the world. The large shrimp which are used for food and bait are salt water species. The six most common species are all members of the *Penaeidae* family – characterized by having the first three pairs of walking legs end in small pincers. Shrimp can be divided into two principal sections: (1) the head, which bears the head spine or rostrum, eyes, antennae, mouthparts and five pairs of walking legs; and (2) abdomen or tail containing seven segments with swimming legs beneath the first five abdominal segments and telson, or tail, on the last segment.

The six most common species of shrimp include: brown shrimp, *Penaeus aztecus;* pink shrimp, *Penaeus duorarum;* white shrimp, *Penaeus setiferus;* sea bob, *Xiphopeneus kroyeri;* rock shrimp, *Sicyonia brevirostris;* royal red shrimp, *Hymenopenaeus robustus.* Colors vary widely – dark and light shades of brown, pink, yellow, gray, white, and red.

In the Gulf of Mexico, white shrimp spawn offshore in 10-15 fathoms of water. The female (which is larger at maturity than the male) lays 500,000 eggs. Spawning season lasts from March to September with the peaks in May-June and August-September. During mating, the male attaches a spermatophore (sperm sac) to the female and the eggs are fertilized as they are laid. The eggs sink to the bottom and after hatching they pass through twelve or more larval and postlarval stages. During these stages, the young are not capable of much movement and are carried by the currents.

Juvenile white shrimp, ¼ inch long, will migrate along the bottom close to shore, preferring mud bottoms and brackish waters. They grow rapidly at the rate of 1¼ inches per month. After reaching 3½ inches, they migrate from their nursery grounds into deeper bays near the ocean. When they reach 4½ to 6 inches, they are mature and move to spawning grounds in the open ocean.

Habits of other shrimp are similar. The brown shrimp spawns in deeper water than the white shrimp, but brown and white shrimps are most common in shallow waters and bays. The pink shrimp is abundant in warm waters in the Tortugas and southwestern Gulf of Mexico. The royal red shrimp occurs primarily in deep water (175-300 fathoms) off the edge of the Continental Shelf.

Food shrimp are concentrated in the southeastern United States along the south Atlantic and Gulf coasts. Commercially, the majority of all catches are taken with ottertrawls. The sport shrimper can catch shrimp with landing nets. The shrimp can be caught off bridges and seawalls.

PREPARATION AND RECIPE

Shrimp are sold by size or grade based on the number of *headless* shrimp per pound: jumbo = 15 or less/pound; small = 60 or more/pound. Freshly caught shrimp must be deheaded immediately. Within the head, the pancreas secretes a substance immediately upon death which dissolves and rots the flesh. Fresh, deheaded shrimp should be cooked within two days of purchase. Fresh shrimp can be frozen in a block of ice or glazed. Raw shrimp will maintain quality, if frozen at 0° F or below, for six months. Cooked shrimp begin deteriorating after one month. Frozen shrimp should be thawed in refrigerator, *not* at room temperature. After thawing, do not *refreeze*.

Cleaning is easier if shrimp are raw: (1) Holding tail in one hand, peel off the shell segments, except the tail. (2) If tail is to be removed, squeeze tail with thumb and forefinger while pulling the shrimp meat with the other hand. (3) Remove the

Shrimp

Commercial shrimp fishermen, Fernandina, Florida

Fisherman separates landed shrimp from crabs, fish, and mollusks

Salt water shrimp

33

"sand vein" – black vein located along upper curve – by making a ⅛ inch cut along the curve and rinsing the vein away under cold running water.

12. Shrimp Creole (4 to 6 servings)

2 pounds shelled and deveined shrimp	3 peeled and cored ripe tomatoes
3 tablespoons butter or bacon drippings	1 bay leaf
	½ teaspoon thyme
	salt
2 cups chopped onions	½ teaspoon black pepper
2 cloves of garlic, finely chopped	¼ teaspoon cayenne pepper
3 pieces celery, chopped	1 teaspoon Worcestershire sauce
1 chopped green pepper	(optional)

Melt butter or drippings in large saucepan and add onions, celery, garlic, green pepper, and cook until tender without browning. Then add tomatoes, bay leaf, thyme, pepper, cayenne, and salt to taste. Simmer for ten minutes with occasional stirring. Add shrimp, cover and simmer ten minutes. Season with Worcestershire if desired and serve with hot rice.

Lobster or scallops can be substituted for shrimp in this recipe. Also see Recipes **9, 23, 25** which can be made with shrimp.

Rock Shrimp *Sicyonia breviostris*

The rock shrimp is a true shrimp but it is treated individually because it is less common and perhaps the best of the family. They are named for their hard lobster-like shell and the meat is similar in texture to the lobster, but the flavor is somewhere between shrimp and lobster. Rock shrimp can be substituted in any recipe which calls for shrimp or lobster.

This species is much more perishable than either shrimp or lobster. Therefore, the heads should be removed immediately after catching and the tails frozen within 24 hours. Most rock shrimp are commercially available as raw frozen tails. They are graded 21-25 per pound, and two pounds of green tails will produce one pound of cooked and peeled shrimp.

PREPARATION AND RECIPE

To clean rock shrimp for steaming: (1) Hold the tail section in one hand while inserting sharp kitchen shears at the top of the shell, cutting through the outer curve to the end of the tail. (2) Pull shell apart and remove flesh. Wash in cold water to remove sand vein. **To clean shrimp for broiling whole tails:** (1) Place shrimp on cutting board "belly up." Using a sharp knife cut between the pairs of swimmerets through the meat to the hard shell. (2) Spread the shell until it lies flat; wash thoroughly in cold running water to remove sand vein.

13. Rock Shrimp Conga (makes 30 hors d'oeuvres)
½ pound raw, peeled and deveined shrimp
2 tablespoons lime juice
½ teaspoon salt
¼ teaspoon pepper
4 tablespoons melted butter or margarine
1½ ounces cream cheese
½ ounce Roquefort or blue cheese

Place rock shrimp in a single layer in a 1½ quart shallow baking dish. Sprinkle shrimp with lime juice, salt and pepper. Cream together cooled melted butter, cream cheese and Roquefort or blue cheese. Spread the mixture over the shrimp. Cover with aluminum foil, folding over the edges of the dish. Bake in hot, 400° F oven for 8-10 minutes.

Also see Recipes **9, 12, 23, 25, 27** which can be made with rock shrimp.

Shrimp boat fleet, Key West, Florida

Headless rock shrimp

Shrimp trawler

Abalone *Haliotis rufescens*

Abalones are large single-shelled mollusks common to the California coast. There are eight different species located from British Columbia to Mexico in Pacific waters, and more than 100 species worldwide. The flat single dish-like shell has an iridescent underside and 4-6 openings through which the animal expels water and wastes. The shells are usually covered by marine growth including algae, barnacles, sponges and hydroids. They can move forward on a single foot at surprising speed when threatened. The abalone's final defense is to withdraw and clamp itself to the substrate. They adhere very strongly to the rocks and must be removed with a pry-bar.

Abalones live in shallow water on rocks, but a few have been found living in water over 1000 feet deep. Adult abalones roam the same area all of their lives. They are vegetarians, feeding mainly on algae and kelp. Besides man, they are threatened by crabs, octopuses, fishes and the sea otters. The sea otter smashes the shell of a clinging abalone with a rock, and scoops out the flesh with its paw.

There are eight species of abalones common in the Pacific waters. The red abalone, *H. rufescens,* is supposedly the best tasting and is fairly common from Washington to California. Minimum size for legal capture of the red abalone is 7

Red abalone   Photo B. Evans

inches. The pink abalone, *H. corrugata,* is fairly common in Southern California; black abalone, *H. cracherodi,* is common from Oregon to Baja California; pinto abalone, *H. kamtschatkana,* fairly common from southern Alaska to central California; northern green abalone, *H. walallensis,* fairly common from British Columbia to California; green abalone, *H. fulgens,* is uncommon, found from Oregon to Baja California; white abalone, *H. sorenseni,* is uncommon but excellent tasting, ranges from Southern California to Baja California; threaded abalone, *H. assimilis,* rare, ranges from Southern California to Baja California.

In California, abalones spawn in the spring and summer. The male abalone ejects sperm and the female abalone ejects eggs which meet in the water. After hatching, the larvae are free-swimming for about 10 days at which time they settle to the bottom to develop into miniature adults over the next 60 days. The red abalone reaches a size of one inch in about one year. It reaches sexual maturity in about four years and five inches in length. Abalones can live 15-20 years and reach lengths of 12 inches.

The abalones are heavily fished commercially – three million pounds of meat a year are harvested.

Sportsmen take abalone by diving for them. State laws control harvesting and restrict legal size. Through modern freezing techniques, abalone steaks are available throughout the United States.

PREPARATION AND RECIPE

When the abalone is harvested, it should be kept in sea water until removed from the shell. The meat should be sliced into filets and *pounded* to break down and tenderize the tissue and release the flavor. After pounding, abalone steaks can be washed and frozen.

14. Abalone Steaks

Combine ⅓ cup flour, ½ teaspoon salt, ⅛ teaspoon pepper. Heat 2 tablespoons olive oil and 1 tablespoon butter or margarine in pan. Beat 1 egg.

Flour abalone steak lightly. Dip in egg, then again in flour. Fry in oil and butter in hot pan or griddle (350° F) for ¾ to 1 minute – NOT MORE THAN ONE MINUTE – on each side. Serve immediately.

Conch *Strombus gigas*

There are about 50 species of conchs, but this section is limited to the pink or queen conch which is a delicacy throughout the Bahamas and the Florida Keys. Early settlers of the Florida Keys believed that eating fresh conch would give them perpetual youth. Natives of Key West still proudly call themselves "conchs" after the shellfish.

The queen conch is a univalve which moves by means of a single foot. They have a horny operculum for defense which covers the opening of the shell when the snail is fully withdrawn. Conchs have two eyes perched at the end of short stalks which branch from the tentacles. The sexes are separate and the females lay long jelly-like strands of eggs. They feed on red algae and can be found in 2-30 feet of water on sand and eel grass. Queen conchs can exceed 15 inches in length across the shell. They are harvested with hooks or nets or are taken by hand.

PREPARATION AND RECIPE

Conch flesh can be cooked, or marinated and eaten raw. Conch meat is naturally tough and must be pounded before eating. Cook conchs by scrubbing the shells with a brush and dropping them into boiling water. Cover and simmer for about 30 minutes to one hour until part of the body protrudes from the shell. Drain and cover with cold water. Remove the meat from the shell and skin off the hard outer cover and remove the intestinal vein. The meat can then be cut and pounded.

To remove raw meat from conch shell: (1) Wash the shells. (2) Crack the base of two shells together to crack them; if this doesn't work, crack the shell with a hammer. (3) With knife and fingers remove flesh from the interior. (4) Cut off the soft matter and the horny clawlike structure attached to the meat. (5) Slit the outer covering of the meat and skin off; remove the intestinal vein. The meat can be cut or ground if it is used in chowder.

15. Conch Seviche (4 servings)

5-8 conchs
1 small peeled and chopped red onion
½ cup fresh lime or lemon juice
2 small tomatoes, peeled, cored and chopped
1 small hot green pepper, finely chopped
salt
pepper
peanut oil

Split cleaned conch flesh down the middle without cutting in half. Pound the flesh lightly but firmly with a heavy mallet. Slice meat into thin slivers and place in bowl with other ingredients using 3 or more tablespoons of peanut oil; salt and pepper to taste. Toss and chill.

Also see Recipe **20** which can be made with conch.

Queen conch

Bahamian fisherman nets conch in shallow waters.

Conch beds in Bahamian waters

Squid *Loligo opalescens*

Unlike the giant species featured in *20,000 Leagues Under the Sea*, the commercial squid is usually less than 12 inches long, although the monsters can grow to 60 feet. Squids are mollusks of the class *Cephalapoda* which are characterized by having large heads and well developed eyes, a tubular funnel on the underside, horny beak-like jaws, and 8-10 arms. There are more than 350 species of squid worldwide. Squids have 10 arms (the octopus has eight) connected to a long body that ends in fins. The mantle covers the entire body and is open only at the head. The body support is a semi-rigid, thin, transparent shell or pen located beneath the mantle of the body. The arms are covered with suction cups and, in some species, with horny, toothed disks or hooks which can be used for holding prey. The tentacles, two of the ten arms, are long and retractable and are used to seize food.

The squid can rapidly propel itself "jet-like" backwards or forwards by drawing water into its mantle and expelling it through a funnel, the siphon, beneath the mantle. Some species can reach speeds of 30 mph. When threatened, the squid

41

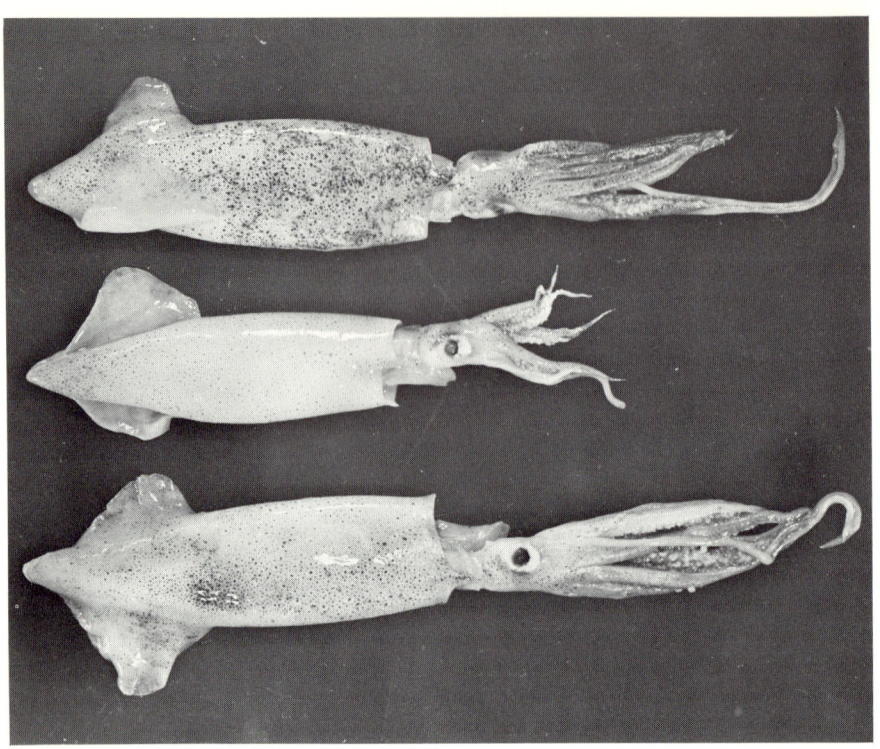

Squid

immediately turns a dark color after which he ejects a cloud of ink approximating his own size and shape. The squid shoots through this camouflage, and when the predator attacks, he finds only a blob of ink which disperses on contact, clouding the water and confusing the predator even more.

Squid are found near the surface down to depths of one mile. They are voracious and feed on fishes and other squids. Small squid, often only an inch in length, travel in schools while very large individuals tend to be solitary travelers.

L. opalescens is common along the west coast of North America. Large schools spawn in shallow waters like those near Catalina Island or near Monterey Bay. Male squids have a "hectocotylus" at the end of one of the arms which is used to transfer sperm to inside the female. After mating, the female lays long strands containing eggs encased in a gelatin-like substance. The egg masses are attached to some rigid object on the sea floor. The young hatch as miniature adults.

Squid are the natural diet of large fish like tunas and marlins, whales and birds. Commercial fishermen use seines, trawlers, traps, gigs, and lights to catch them.

PREPARATION AND RECIPE

Dressing squid: (1) Cut through arms and tentacles near the eyes. (2) Discard the inedible beak which is located near the cut. (3) Hold the body under running water and peel off the thin outer skin. (4) Feel inside and pull out the stiff pen and attached viscera and head. (5) Wash in cold water and dry on paper towels. Squid can be left whole for stuffing, cut into rings, or cut into bite size pieces by slitting down one side to open the squid flat for cutting.

16. Baked Stuffed Squid (6-8 servings)   by Mary Alongi

2 pounds squid, cleaned and skinned
½ cup melted butter or margarine
2 cups soft bread crumbs
1 teaspoon minced garlic
¾ teaspoon salt
¼ teaspoon black pepper
1 pound canned tomatoes
1 cup dry white wine (optional)

Chop arms and tentacles and combine with bread crumbs, garlic, salt and pepper, melted margarine or butter. Mix well. Stuff squid with bread mixture, closing the opening with round wooden toothpicks. Place stuffed squid in baking dish and pour tomatoes and wine *or* butter and lemon sauce (melt ¼ pound butter or margarine and combine with ½ cup lemon juice) over squid. Bake in 350° F oven for 30-40 minutes.

Also see Recipe **20** which can be made with squid.

Blue Mussel   *Mytilus edulis*

Mussels are found world-wide but are most abundant in cool waters. There are 40 species in U.S. waters. Most have pear shaped shells which are thin and strong and have a high gloss interior. Some have small weak hinge teeth, others do not. Mussels are sedentary and fix themselves to rocks by long silky filaments called the byssus. The young mussel is free-swimming and even the adult is not permanently anchored.

The blue mussel is found in waters from the Arctic ocean to South Carolina and in California. It is particularly abundant in New England. The mussel has a bluish-black shell, for which it is named, is very common and found in quiet, shallow waters attached to rocks and pilings in crowded colonies in the intertidal zones. At certain times mussels contain a toxic substance released by algae concentrated in the gill cavities. Certain areas have laws prohibiting harvesting and eating mussels in summer months when this toxicity is more prevalent.

When mussels are in medium depth waters they can be harvested by long handled tongs. In shallow waters, they can be pried loose by hand. Do not collect mussels exposed by low tide during summer months. You may collect dead mussels along with live shellfish. Like clams and oysters, live mussels clamp their shells shut when handled. The best tasting mussels are harvested in fall through early spring. The mussels spawn in late spring and early summer and are lean and watery at this time.

Blue mussels

Blue mussels

PREPARATION AND RECIPE

Discard all mussels with open shells. Each mussel must be individually scrubbed to remove mud and growth on shells. The byssus or "beard" must be trimmed with a knife. Wash in running water to remove sand. They can be steamed and eaten like steamed clams.

17. Moules Poulette

3 dozen cleaned and washed mussels	3 egg yolks
2 shallots, chopped	½ pound heavy cream
6 mushrooms thinly sliced (optional)	1 tablespoon parsley, chopped
1 cup white wine	salt
¼ pound butter or margarine	pepper

In a covered saucepan, steam mussels in 2 cups of water and wine for 6-8 minutes. After shell has opened place mussels on half of the shell in a flat dish. Strain the liquid and save. In another pan add chopped shallots and mushrooms and brown in the butter or margarine. Add flour, strained mussel juice, stirring continually until the sauce is partially thickened. Add egg yolks, cream, and parsley until sauce is well blended. Correct the seasoning with salt and pepper. Pour sauce over cooked mussels and serve hot.

Clams

Most all species of clams are good to eat, but some kinds may be bitter. However, when collecting clams on your own, be sure you take only those from waters surveyed by local health authorities. Depending on their environment, clams can be toxic or even deadly. Clams – and oysters, scallops and mussels – can become toxic due to occurrence of poisonous plankton blooms (such as Red Tide) or from pollution by untreated sewage. Some varieties of hepatitis can come from eating raw clams that have become toxic. Commercial supplies must pass rigid inspection laws.

Clams are salt water mollusks. Fresh water bivalves are called "clams" but are really mussels.

Methods of reproduction and larval development vary greatly with the various classes and families of mollusks. The sexes may be separate, or the individuals may be hermaphroditic, or they may even change sexes at some point in their development. Clams produce eggs and sperm in gonads which pass the cells either into the kidney tube or into the mantle cavity. The eggs may be fertilized in open sea water or within the animal.

They grow by adding new shell material around the outside. These growth rings are the result of environment and even though they may correspond to seasons, they do not necessarily indicate age. Warm water increases growth rate.

Maryland clam fishermen Photo M. E. Warren

The more common and popular clams are detailed. However other good eating clams include the bean clam, *Donax* sp. which is popular in soups; the cockles, which can be used in stews and chowders; and the surf or skimmer clam, *Polynyma solidissima* which is popular for use in chowders.

Soft-shell Clam *Mya arenaria*

The soft-shell clam, also known as "longneck" and "steamer" clam, is a member of the family *Myacidae* characterized by the long retractable siphons which are contained in a single, long tube.

They are common and are found on the Atlantic Coast from Labrador to South Carolina, on the western coast of Florida and the central coast of California. Soft-shell clams can be found in sandy mud and under stones, primarily in the intertidal zone.

This species is considered a delicacy particularly when eaten raw. The steamer clam is commercially fished and many end up in cans.

Cherrystone Clam   *Mercenaria mercenaria*

The cherrystone is also commonly known as "quahog" and "hard-shell" clam. It is a member of the family *Veneridae* – Venus clams – having egg or heart shaped shells and are equivalve. There are a dozen species of Venus clams in American waters, most of which are found in shallow waters and protected bays. The cherrystone clam inhabits waters from Canada to Florida and has been introduced in California waters.

Sub-species include the Texas quahog, *M. m. texana,* found in the western Gulf of Mexico, and *M. m. notata* which is marked with brown zig-zag lines and found in the same area as *M. mercenaria.*

Hard-shells are commonly found in shallow waters 1-6 fathoms deep. They spawn during a period of months when tide fluctuation is small and when the tide is out. Larvae swim on the sea floor to find mud covered hard surfaces. The larvae secrete a byssus to attach themselves where they remain until the siphons develop – about a week. Their natural enemies include crabs, snails and other crustaceans.

The hard-shell is harvested commercially by hand operated clam rakes or by using hydraulic dredge boats. The boats unearth buried clams with high pressure jets of water. The clams are then picked up with rakes.

The Pacific littleneck clam, *Protothaca staminea,* found from Alaska to Baja California, is a related west coast species which is good eating and commercially marketed as hard-shell clams.

Cherrystone clams are eaten more often in cooked and chowder forms than is the soft-shell clam.

Pacific Geoduck   *Panope generosa*

This is the largest species of American clam. The shell can reach up to nine inches across and have siphons up to two feet long. The siphons cannot be completely withdrawn. It is an excellent eating clam, including the siphons. Some states impose a daily limit on the number that can be taken.

The Pacific geoduck is common, found in two or three feet of mud from Alaska to Baja California.

PREPARATION AND RECIPES
How to shuck a clam: (1) Over a bowl, hold clam in one hand with hinged side against palm; insert knife blade between shells. (2) Holding the shell firmly, cut around the opening twisting the knife up slightly to pry the shell open. (3) Using your thumb, lift the top shell. (4) Cut the muscle free from both halves, serving the meat in the deep half or store muscle and juices in container in shucked form.

Soft-shell clams

Cherrystone clams

Pacific geoduck

18. Steamed Clams

Thoroughly wash soft-shell clams in the shell. If these clams have been dug out of the sand soak them in salt water (⅓ cup salt to 1 gallon water) for 15 minutes. Rinse and repeat.

Place cleaned clams on raised rack in bottom of tightly closing pot containing one cup hot water. Steam until shells just open – about one minute. Discard any clams that do not open. Serve in shells with drawn butter and heated clam juice. The skin covering the siphon is too tough to eat and can be rolled off before dipping the clam. As a main dish, allow 15-20 clams per person.

19. Clams Oreganato by Estelle Bruscato

18 hard shell clams
¼ pound butter or margarine
½ onion, diced
1 or 2 garlic buds, minced
chopped parsley
lemons
1-1½ cups seasoned bread crumbs commercially available (or make your own with oregano and parmesan cheese, paprika, salt and pepper to taste)

Save clam juice; finely chop clams. In a skillet, melt the butter, add the onion, parsley, and garlic and saute for 5-10 minutes. Add bread crumbs until all butter is absorbed and add one tablespoon of the clam juice.

Place chopped clams on one half of shell and squeeze fresh lemon over each clam. Pack bread crumb mixture over each clam to fill the shell. Bake about 10 minutes in 400° F oven, and then brown under broiler for about 1 minute. Serve hot.

20. New England Clam Chowder (6 servings)

24 medium clams in shell or 1 pint shucked clams
¼ pound chopped salt pork
4 cups peeled and diced potatoes
½ cup chopped onion
2 cups milk
1 cup light cream
3 tablespoons flour
1½ teaspoons salt
pepper

To open clams in shell, place in steamer with one cup water. Cover and bring water to boil. Lower heat and continue steaming until shells open, 5-10 minutes. Remove clams from shells; strain and save ½ cup liquid.

Mince or grind clams. Fry salt pork until crisp; remove and hold the bits of pork. Add ½ cup clam juice, 1½ cups water, potatoes, onion, to pork fat; cover and cook about 15-20 minutes until potatoes are tender. Add clams, 1¾ cups of the milk and the cream. Mix the remaining milk with the flour and stir into the chowder. Cook until boiling, while stirring. Add salt and pepper to taste; sprinkle with the pork bits.

Squid, conch, oysters, scallops or mussels can be substituted for clams in the chowder recipe. Also see Recipes **22, 23** which can be made with clams.

Oysters   Family *Ostreidae*

There are several kinds of edible oysters in the family *Ostreidae*, but those in American waters are in two genera, *Ostrea* and *Crassostrea*. The shapes of the oysters vary greatly and are directly influenced by the environment. Pearls produced by the edible oysters are not lustrous and are of little value.

Natural oyster beds are usually located in river mouths and bays where water salinity is reduced. They are normally found in intertidal regions to 40-50 feet in brackish waters. The oysters may grow in deeper waters, but they are not commercially valuable. Oysters adapt easily to changes in temperature and water salinity.

Crassostrea lays eggs directly into the sea where they are fertilized by sperm which has been released by the male. *Ostrea* incubates eggs within the mantle cavity. Individual oysters are of one sex, but sex reversal is common. Eggs are produced in summer and develop into small larvae covered with cilia. The larva is free swimming for a period of 1-3 weeks until it develops a small foot and cements itself to some agreeable hard surface (usually oyster shells) and is known as a "spat." Oysters reach edible size in three years under normal conditions. A female lays approximately 50 million eggs in one season but only 10-12 reach maturity. Foes of the oyster include starfish, crabs, oyster drill snails; many are killed by a parasitic fungus.

If you harvest oysters yourself, be sure to check with local health authorities to make sure waters are not polluted.

American oysters

American Oyster *Crassostrea virginica*

The American oyster, or eastern oyster as it is sometimes called, is widely distributed and very abundant. It ranges from New Brunswick to the Gulf of Mexico and thrives in the inshore waters of the Atlantic and Gulf coasts, where the salinity of the waters is reduced. The oysters are highly concentrated in Chesapeake Bay and on the west coast of Florida.

The American oyster is the most popular and most flavorful of the edible oysters. They grow to market size in 2-5 years depending on water temperature and salinity. Sex reversal in this species is common; one year old oysters are male and then they switch to females.

They are harvested with hand tongers if beds are shallow or by commercial patent tongers.

American oyster

Native Pacific oyster

Giant Pacific oyster

Oystermen with long tongs harvest Apalachicola Bay's most valuable seafood crop.

Native Pacific Oyster   *Ostrea lurida*

This species is also known as the Olympia oyster. It is generally small but highly valued as food; the shell seldom exceeds 2½ inches. They are slow growing and require 4-5 years to reach market size.

It is common in the intertidal zones on the Pacific coast from British Columbia to San Diego Harbor, California. The oyster is highly concentrated in Puget Sound, Washington.

They are harvested commercially by use of a dike system used to produce pools out of mud flats. In this set-up tide levels are controlled so that larvae are allowed to hatch and remain for a year or two before being moved.

Giant Pacific Oyster   *Crassostrea gigas*

This species is common on the Pacific coast from Canada to California and is native to Japan.

This Chesapeake Bay Skipjack sail boat is one of a remaining fleet of 31 boats which are used by commercial oystermen to dredge for oysters. The sail boats were the result of an 1865 Maryland conservation law which required that oyster dredging had to be done by sail instead of power boats.
Photo Ted Hopkins

The oyster is introduced yearly as seed in California during February and March, and left undisturbed until the following spring. The oyster will propagate naturally in American waters but not consistently if water temperatures are too cold.

The giant Pacific oyster grows rapidly to market size in less than two years. This rapid growth is a handicap since the oyster is often too large for trade consumption. It is well suited for canning but inferior to the American oyster in appearance and flavor and is not served raw on the half shell.

The inability to spawn under certain temperature conditions leaves large egg masses within the oyster which will ruin its flavor.

PREPARATION AND RECIPES

Oysters must be alive when in the shell – they close their shells tightly when handled.

How to shuck an oyster: Cotton gloves should be worn to protect the hands. Use an oyster knife – a heavy wedge-shaped blade designed to take the pressure required to open oysters. Don't use a sharp knife. After scrubbing the shells and washing the oysters thoroughly: (1) Hold the oyster by the thin end leaving the hinge portion exposed. (2) Insert the knife in crevice between the shells at the hinge, twisting the knife while pushing to break the hinge. (3) After hinge is broken, but before pulling shells apart, slide the knife along inside of the top shell to cut the muscle loose from the shell. (4) Remove the top shell, and cut oyster away from bottom shell, being careful not to mutilate the oyster. (5) Remove any shell particles from the oyster.

Very large oysters may require that the thin part (away from the hinge) be broken with a hammer in order to open the shell. This will leave shell particles in the flesh which should be removed.

If the shucking process becomes too much for you, place the oysters in a 400° F oven for 5-7 minutes depending on size. Put them into ice water very briefly and drain. They should now open easily, however some of the flavor will have been lost.

Oysters will remain live in the shell in the refrigerator for 7-10 days if stored un-iced at 35° F to 40° F. Freshly shucked oysters, if packed in ice, can be stored in the refrigerator for about a week without losing quality. Oysters lose considerable quality during home freezing and this is not recommended. Commercially frozen oysters are "quick frozen" and these are fine.

Serve oysters raw on the half shell after chilling. Place on cracked ice in serving dish and serve with hot cocktail sauce.

21. Oysters Rockefeller

24 oysters in shell or 1 pint shucked oysters
2 tablespoons chopped parsley
1 tablespoon chopped onion
1 tablespoon melted butter or margarine
1 cup cooked chopped spinach
¼ cup fine dry bread crumbs
½ cup butter or margarine
paprika
salt
pepper

Shuck and drain oysters. Wash shells and place each oyster in deep half of the shell. Combine parsley, onion, 1 tablespoon melted butter, and spread mixture over oysters. Sprinkle with paprika, salt and pepper to taste. On top of each oyster place 2 teaspoons of the chopped spinach and ½ teaspoon of bread crumbs. Place about 1 teaspoon butter or margarine on top of each oyster. Bake over a bed of rock salt until browned, about 10 minutes in 460° F oven.

22. Oysters Casino

24 oysters in shells, or 1 pint shucked oysters
¼ cup softened butter or margarine
¼ cup chopped green onion
¼ cup chopped green pepper
¼ cup finely chopped celery
2 tablespoons chopped pimento
1 teaspoon lemon juice
4 slices bacon, cooked until crisp and crumbled
salt

Shuck and drain oysters. Wash shell and place each oyster in deep half of the shell. Salt lightly. Combine remaining ingredients and cover each oyster with about a tablespoon of the topping. Bake over a bed of rock salt at 425° F for 10-12 minutes.

Clams can be substituted for oysters in this recipe.

23. Fried Oysters

Drain oysters and dry on paper towels. Dredge oysters in mixture of all-purpose flour seasoned with salt and pepper. Dip oyster into mixture of 1 beaten egg and 1 tablespoon water and then in fine bread crumbs. Deep-fry for about 2 minutes in hot fat (375° F) or until golden brown. Serve hot with tartar sauce or cocktail sauce.

Clams, shrimp, or scallops can be substituted for oysters in this recipe. See Recipe **20** which can be made with oysters.

Hand tonger with oysters

Scallops   Family *Pectinidae*

The true scallops are all in the family *Pectinidae* and include many species of commercially important edible scallops. Most of the 50 species of American scallops can be classified in seven genera.

Scallops are good swimmers — they propel themselves by opening and suddenly closing the two shells, creating a jet of water. By varying the position of the escaping water, the scallop can control its direction of movement. In normal swimming movements, the scallop opens and closes the valves forcing water out on both sides of the hinge which propels the scallop forward. Movement of the bivalve shell is accomplished by the single adductor muscle which is fixed on one end by an elastic ligament.

Scallops have well developed eyes — some species have as many as 100 — positioned along the edge of the mantle. They also have small tentacles along the edge of the mantle which are sensitive to odor and change in water pressure and movement.

Sexes can be separate or scallops can be hermaphroditic. They spawn in spring depositing eggs and sperm directly into the water. Larvae are free-swimming for a period ranging from several days to a few weeks after which time the young scallops attach themselves by thin filaments, produced by the foot. Scallops can be free or stationary like the oyster, but most adults are free. Sexual maturity is reached at two years and the scallop may live 5-6 years.

Calico scallops

The sportsman can get better quality scallops himself than those normally marketed. Commercial distributors will often soak scallops in fresh water until the adductor muscle becomes plump and white but this also diminishes the flavor.

Scallops can be taken by hand rakes and more easily by net. Permits or licenses are required by most areas and legal harvesting size is also regulated.

Atlantic Deep Sea Scallop *Placopecten magellanicus*

This very large and common scallop is found on the Atlantic coast from Labrador to North Carolina. It is found in 20-300 feet of water.

The deep sea scallop is dredged throughout the year. More than 30 million pounds are harvested annually, mostly off Massachusetts. The scallop is shucked and iced at sea.

Calico Scallop *Aequipecten gibbus*

This species is a commercial scallop of the southeast United States and is the basis of a large fishery in Florida. It is common in 6-30 feet of water and is harvested on trawlers which bring the scallops to shore where they are shucked and iced.

The scallop muscle is ½ to ¾ inches in diameter.

Atlantic Bay Scallop *Aequipecten irradians*

The range of the bay scallop is from Nova Scotia to New Jersey. It has two sub-species: *A. i. concentricus* found from New Jersey to Georgia and Tampa Bay to Los Angeles; and *A. i. amplicostatus* which is common in Texas and ranges from Texas to Colombia, South America.

The species is common and found in eel grass.

Giant Pacific Scallop *Pecten caurinus*

This species is found off the Pacific coast from Alaska to California. It is commercially fished in offshore waters up to 200 feet deep.

PREPARATION AND RECIPES

Only the round adductor muscle of the scallop is eaten. Scallops cannot close their shells tightly and as a result they die soon after being removed from the water. The scallops must be shucked and iced immediately after they are harvested. When purchased in packages, either fresh or frozen, the scallops should be practically free of liquid. Fresh scallops can be white, light tan or pinkish and will have a mild slightly sweet odor. Shucked fresh scallops can be stored on ice in a refrigerator at 35°-40° F for about two days. Raw, frozen scallops can be held at 0° F or below for 3-4 months.

How to shuck a scallop: (1) Hold scallop in one hand with hinge against the palm. Using a strong, slender – not sharp – knife, insert the blade between the shells near the hinge, twisting to gain access to the inside. Do not force shell open. (2) Lift the top shell far enough to insert the knife point and sever the muscle from the top shell. Remove the top shell. (3) Remove the viscera from the bottom shell by gripping the dark portion of the scallop between the thumb and knife blade and pulling gently. This should remove everything except the edible white scallop muscle. (4) After the viscera is removed cut the muscle from the bottom shell. Wash the meat and place in moisture proof wrapping and ice immediately.

24. Baked Scallops (6 servings)

2 pounds scallops
2 cups rich butter cracker crumbs
¼ cup melted margarine or butter
¼ cup catsup
½ teaspoon salt
¼ teaspoon sugar
pepper
¼ cup sliced green onions and tops
1 tablespoon melted margarine
  or butter
paprika

Rinse thawed scallops with cold water to remove any shell particles. Cut any large scallops in half. Combine scallops, cracker crumbs, margarine, catsup, salt, sugar and pepper. Divide scallop mixture into 6 well greased 10-ounce casseroles. Combine green onion and margarine and place on top of scallop mixture. Bake in oven at 350° F for 25-30 minutes or until brown. Sprinkle with paprika if desired.

25. Scallops Teriyaki (4 servings)

1 pound scallops
½ cup soy sauce
¼ cup dry sherry
2 tablespoons sugar
2 tablespoons olive oil
¾ teaspoon ground ginger
1 clove garlic, crushed

Rinse thawed scallops and cut any large ones in half. Place in shallow dish. Combine remaining ingredients and pour over scallops. Let scallops marinate for 30 minutes at room temperature. Drain the scallops and hold the marinade. Impale scallops on four skewers and place on shallow greased baking pan. Bake for 15 minutes at 450° F turning and basting with marinade. Sprinkle with chopped parsley if desired.

Shrimp can be substituted for scallops in this recipe.

26. Bouillabaisse (6-8 servings)

1 pound lobster meat in shell
1 pound red snapper fillets
  or sole fillets
1 pound other fish fillets (cod, haddock, flounder, bass)
12 ounces scallops
12 clams in shell
2 large onions, chopped
⅓ cup olive oil
4 cups chopped cored tomato

Atlantic deep sea scallop

Calico scallops

Atlantic bay scallop

Giant Pacific scallop

Commercial scallop fisherman shovels a fresh catch into bushels for shucking.

1 clove garlic, minced
2 sprigs parsley
1 bay leaf
1 teaspoon dried crushed
 thyme leaves (optional)
¼ teaspoon crushed saffron
 (optional)
salt
pepper
French bread

Thaw frozen shellfish and fish. Split lobsters in shell into 6-8 portions; cut fish fillets into 2-inch pieces; cut any large scallops in half. Wash clams thoroughly. Pour oil in large saucepan and add onion and cook until tender but not browned. Add 6 cups water or fish stock, tomato, garlic, parsley, bay leaf, thyme, saffron, 1 tablespoon salt and dash pepper. Cover and simmer for 30 minutes. Strain stock into large pot; discard the vegetables and herbs.

Bring the strained stock to a boil and add lobster and fish; cook for 5 minutes. Add scallops and clams and continue boiling until clams open, about 5 minutes. Serve with French bread.

Appendix
Shellfish Sauces

27. Newburg
This sauce can be served with lobster, scallops, crab or shrimp.

6 tablespoons butter or margarine
2 tablespoons all-purpose flour
1½ cups light cream
3 egg yolks, beaten
3 tablespoons dry white wine
2 teaspoons lemon juice
toast points
paprika

In saucepan, melt butter and blend in flour. Add cream. Cook, stirring constantly until sauce thickens and begins to bubble. Stir a small amount of the mixture into the beaten egg yolks and return to saucepan. Cook, stirring constantly until thickened. Add shellfish, cooking until thoroughly heated. Add wine, lemon juice and ¼ teaspoon salt. Serve over toast. Sprinkle with paprika (optional).

28. Cocktail Sauce (makes 1½ cups)
Serve with raw oysters or clams, or with boiled shrimp or crabs.

½ cup catsup
½ cup chili sauce
2 tablespoons horseradish
2 teaspoons Worcestershire sauce
3 dashes Tabasco
½ cup chopped celery
juice of one lemon

Combine all ingredients and chill.

29. Mustard Sauce

See recipe listed under stone crab. This sauce can be served with any steamed crab.

30. Drawn or Clarified Butter

Melt butter over low heat until completely melted. Remove from heat and allow to cool until milk solids settle to bottom. Draw off the clear butter fat from the top. The clarified butter is ready to use.

31. Tartar Sauce (makes one cup)

Can be served with fried shrimp, scallops, oysters, or clams.

1 cup mayonnaise or salad dressing
3 tablespoons finely chopped
    dill pickle
1 tablespoon parsley flakes
2 teaspoons chopped pimento
1 teaspoon grated onion

Combine all ingredients and chill before serving.

Index

Bold numbers refer to photos.
abalone 37-38, **37**
  black 38
  green 38
  northern green 38
  pink 38
  pinto 38
  red 37, **37**
  steaks 38
  threaded 38
  white 38
Aequipecten gibbus 58
Aequipecten irradians 58
American lobster 6-11, **7, 8**
American oyster 51, **51, 52, 53**
Arthropoda 4
Atlantic bay scallop 58, **60**
Atlantic deep sea scallop 58, **60**
au gratin, crab 27
baked scallops 59
baked stuffed lobster 14
baked stuffed squid 43
blue crab 17-22, **17, 19, 20, 22**
  steamed **21**
blue mussel 43-45, **44**
boiled crawfish 16
bouillabaisse 59
broiled lobster 14
byssus 43
Callinectes sapidus 17
calico scallops **57**, 58, **60**
Cambarellus 14
Cambarus 14
Cancer magister 23
cangrejo 5
Cephalopoda 4

cephalopods 5
cherrystone clams 47, **48**
Chesapeake Bay Skipjack **54**
clams 45-50, **46**
  bake 10, **19**
  bean 46
  cherrystone 47, **48**
  chowder 50
  hard-shell 47
  longneck 46
  oreganato 49
  Pacific geoduck 47, **49**
  Pacific littleneck 47
  skimmer 46
  soft-shell 46, **48**
  steamed 49
  steamer 46
  venus 47
clarified butter 63
cocktail sauce 62
conch 39, **40, 41**
  seviche 39
crabs 17-31
  au gratin 27
  blue 17-22, **17, 19, 20, 22**
  Dungeness 23-24, **24**
  fried soft-shell 22
  king 24-28, **25**
  Louis 23
  pot **20, 29**
  snow 27
  soft-shell 18
  stone 28-30, **28, 29**
  stone with mustard sauce 30
crawfish 14-17, **15**
  boiled 16

63

Crassostrea 50
Crassostrea gigas 53
Crassostrea virginica 51
creole, shrimp 34
Crustacea 4
culls 6
Decapoda 4
Donax 46
drawn butter 63
Dungeness crab 23-24, **24**
escargot 5
fried oysters 56
fried soft-shell crabs 22
Gastropoda 4, 5
gastropods 5
giant Pacific scallop 58, **61**
Haliotis assimilis 38
Haliotis corrugata 38
Haliotis cracherodi 38
Haliotis fulgens 38
Haliotis kamtschatkana 38
Haliotis rufescens 37
Haliotis sorenseni 38
Haliotis walallensis 38
hard-shell clam 47
Homarus americanus 6
Hymenopenaeus robustus 31
king crab 24-28, **25**
lobster
   American 6-11, **7, 8**
   baked stuffed 14
   broiled 14
   pot **9, 12**
   spiny 11-14, **12, 13**
   steamed 10
Loligo opalescens 41
longneck clam 46
Louis dressing 24
Menippe mercenaria 28
Mercenaria mercenaria 47
Mercenaria mercenaria notata 47
Mercenaria mercenaria texana 47
Molluska 4
mollusks 5
moules poulette 45
mussel, blue 43-45, **44**
mustard sauce 30
Mya arenaria 46
Myacidae 46
Mytilus edulis 43
native Pacific oyster **52,** 53
Newburg sauce 62
New England clam bake 10
New England clam chowder 50
Orconectes 14
Ostrea 50
Ostrea lurida 53
Ostreidae 50
oysters 50-56, **56**
   American 51, **51, 52,** 53
   casino 55
   fried 56
   giant Pacific **52,** 53
   native Pacific **52,** 53
   Rockefeller 55
Pacifasticus 14

Pacific geoduck **49**
Pacific littleneck clam 47
Panope generosa 47
Panulirus argus 11
Paralithodes camtschatica 24
Pecten caurinus 58
Pectinidae 57
Pelecypoda 4
Penaeidae 31
Penaeus aztecus 31
Penaeus duorarum 31
Penaeus setiferus 31
pink conch 39
pistols
Placopecten magellanicus 58
pod **25**
Polynyma solidissima 46
Procambarus 14
Procambarus blandingi acutus 15
Procambarus clarki 15
Prothothaca staminea 47
queen conch 39, **40**
quahog 47
rock shrimp 34-36, **36**
rock shrimp conga 35
scallops 57-62, **61**
   Atlantic bay 58, **60**
   Atlantic deep sea 58, **60**
   baked 59
   calico **57,** 58, **60**
   giant Pacific 58, **61**
   teriyaki 59
seviche 39
shorts 9
shrimp 31-36, **32, 33**
   brown 31
   creole 34
   pink 31
   rock 31-34, **36**
   royal red 31
   sea bob 31
   trawler **35, 36**
   white 31
Sicyonia brevirostris 31, 34
snappers 9
snow crab 27
soft-shell clam 46, **48**
soft-shell crabs 18
spiny lobster 11-14, **12**
squid 41-43, **42**
squid, baked stuffed 43
steamed blue crabs **21,** 21
steamed clams 49
steamer clam 46
steamed lobster 10
stone crab 28-30, **28, 29**
stone crabs with mustard sauce 30
Strombus gigas 39
tartar sauce 63
teriyaki, scallops 59
Texas quahog 47
Veneridae 47
Venus clams 47
Xanthidae 28
Xiphopeneus kroyeri 31